How do they work?

Playgrounds

Wendy Sadler

Heinemann LIBRARY   Young Explorer

www.heinemann.co.uk/library

Visit our website to find out more information about **Heinemann Library** books.

To order:

 Phone 44 (0) 1865 888066

 Send a fax to 44 (0) 1865 314091

 Visit the Heinemann Bookshop at www.heinemann.co.uk/library to browse our catalogue and order online.

First published in Great Britain by Heinemann Library, Halley Court, Jordan Hill, Oxford OX2 8EJ, part of Harcourt Education.
Heinemann is a registered trademark of Harcourt Education Ltd.

Editorial: Andrew Farrow and Dan Nunn
Design: Ron Kamen and Dave Oakley/
 Arnos Design
Picture Research: Hannah Taylor
Production: Duncan Gilbert
Originated by Ambassador Litho Ltd
Printed and bound in China by
South China Printing Company.

The paper used to print this book comes from sustainable resources.

0 431 04965 3
09 08 07 06 05
10 9 8 7 6 5 4 3 2 1

British Library Cataloguing in Publication Data
Sadler, Wendy

Sadler, Wendy
 Playgrounds. – (How do they work?)
 1. Playgrounds – Equipment and supplies – Juvenile literature
 I. Title
 688.7'6

A full catalogue record for this book is available from the British Library.

Acknowledgements
The publishers would like to thank the following for permission to reproduce photographs:
Alamy Images (Shotfile) p. **4**; Harcourt Education Ltd (Tudor Photography) pp. **5**, **6**, **7**, **8**, **9**, **10**, **11**, **13**, **14**, **15**, **16**, **17**, **18**, **19**, **20**, **21**, **22**, **23**, **24**, **25**, **26**, **27**, **28–29**; Reuters (Simon Kwong) p. **12**.

Cover photograph reproduced with permission of Harcourt Education Ltd (Tudor Photography).

Every effort has been made to contact copyright holders of any material reproduced in this book. Any omissions will be rectified in subsequent printings if notice is given to the publishers.

Contents

Some words are shown in bold, **like this**. You can find out what they mean by looking in the glossary.

 Find out more about playgrounds at
www.heinemannexplore.co.uk

Playgrounds

climbing frame

slides

swings

This is a playground with lots of things to play on. There are slides to slide down and swings to swing on. There is also a climbing **frame** to climb on.

Some playground toys need more
than one person to make them work.
You need two people to play on a
see-saw like this.

Climbing frames

wood

metal

Climbing **frames** can be made of metal, wood, or both. Metal and wood are both strong **materials**. They do not bend when you climb on them.

body twists to fit through gap

You use your hands and feet to pull yourself on to a climbing frame. To get through spaces you need to twist and turn your body.

Climbing ropes

Some climbing **frames** are made of ropes. The ropes move around when you put your **weight** on them. This makes them harder to climb.

ropes

Sometimes you use a rope to help you climb. You pull on the rope to lift yourself up. You must hold the rope tightly so you do not fall down.

9

Slides

A slide is a fun way to move from a high place to a low place. First of all, you need to climb the steps to get to the top.

gravity pulls you down

At the top of a slide you sit down and push off against the edge. A **force** called **gravity** pulls you down towards the ground.

Sliding and stopping

A slide has to be smooth to work. Most slides are made of metal, which is very smooth. Some slides use water to make them **slippery**. Water slides can be very fast!

These children are sliding down a water slide.

To slow down on a slide you push against the sides. Your hands or feet rub against the slide. This makes a **force** called **friction**, which makes you stop.

13

See-saws

push

A see-saw needs two people to work. To start, one person pushes off the ground with their feet. This makes their end of the see-saw go up.

14

push

Each time a person's feet touch the ground they push off again. That person goes up and the other person comes down. Then it is the other person's turn to push off!

15

Heavy and light

child

adult

A see-saw works best if the two people on it are about the same size. This is because a big person is heavier than a small person. A see-saw with one child and one adult on it would not work very well.

the child is light

the adult is heavier

If you play on a see-saw with a bigger person, like an adult, you may get stuck up in the air! The heavier person will get stuck down on the ground.

17

Swings

A swing lets you move forwards and backwards through the air. You sit on the seat and hold on to the ropes or chains. You need to lift your feet off the ground to get moving.

frame

A swing has to be **joined** on to something. Most swings have a **frame** that is stuck to the ground. The ropes or chains join the seat to the frame.

chain

19

Moving on a swing

To make yourself move on a swing you push with your feet. Then you lift your feet off the ground so you can swing forwards.

This girl has pushed back with her feet and is about to lift them off the ground.

push

An adult or a friend can push you on a swing. They need to give you a push at just the right time. If they do not push at the right time, they might get in the way of the swing when it is moving.

Roundabout

fixed in the middle

This is a roundabout. A roundabout is a bit like a wheel. It is fixed in the middle so it can spin around.

push

the roundabout turns this way

To make a roundabout move, you push off against the ground with your feet. Once it is moving you can step on to the roundabout.

23

Stopping a roundabout

a push keeps the roundabout moving

A roundabout needs to be pushed to keep it moving. If you want to go faster, ask the person pushing to push the roundabout harder.

Soon after you stop pushing a roundabout it will slow down and then stop. **Friction** in the roundabout makes this happen.

Always wait until a roundabout stops moving before you get off!

25

Springs

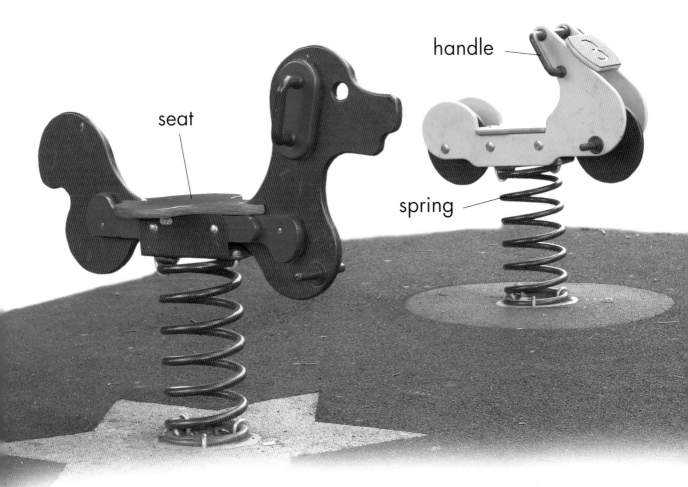

seat

handle

spring

Some playground toys use a giant **spring** to make them move. When you sit on the spring it squashes because of your **weight**. It has a seat to sit on, and handles to hold on to.

You can move a playground spring toy from side to side, or forwards and backwards. The spring always tries to go back to the shape it was at the start.

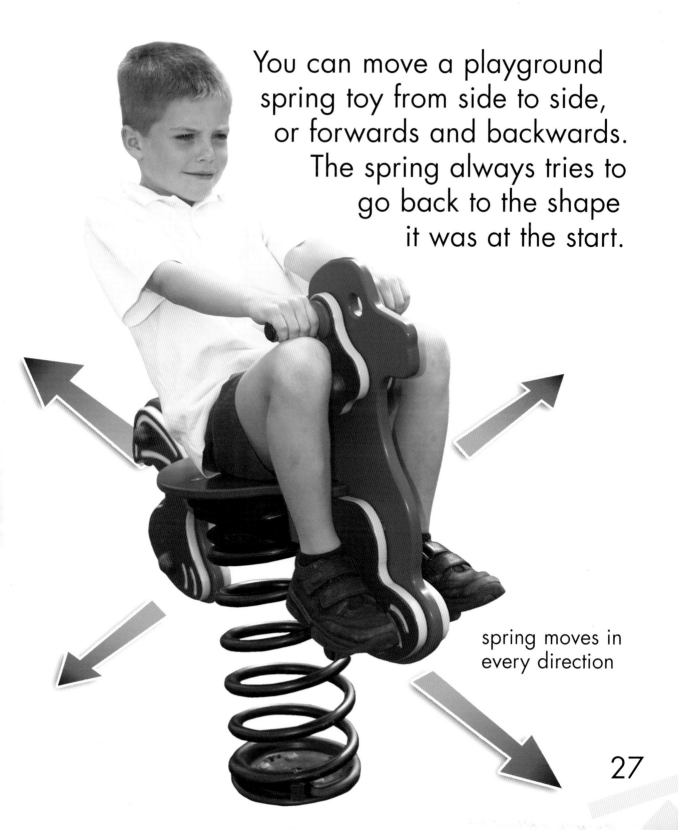

spring moves in every direction

Playground forces

You need lots of **forces** to move in a playground. You need to push and pull things in lots of different ways.

swinging

pulling

turning

pulling

pushing

pushing

29

Glossary

force push or pull that makes something move or keeps it from moving. Gravity and friction are forces.

frame strong shape that holds something up

friction the force of one thing rubbing against another thing. Friction slows things down or stops them moving.

gravity force that pulls things towards the ground. When you jump up, gravity pulls you back to the ground.

joined held together

material something that is used to make things. Plastic, wood, and metal are all types of material.

slippery very smooth

spring piece of metal or plastic curled into loops

weight how heavy something is

Find out more

More books to read

Everyday Science Experiments at the Playground,
John Hartzog (Rosen Publishing, 2000)

Playground Physics: Simple Machines, Bob DeWeese
(Evan-Moor Educational Publishers, 1994)

Playground Science, Elizabeth Paren (Longman, 2004)

Websites to visit

http://www.brainpop.com/science/index.weml
This website has videos and quizzes about gravity and
lots of other science stuff!

http://www.tryscience.org/home.html
Visit this website for lots of simple experiments for you to
try at home.

Disclaimer

All the Internet addresses (URLs) given in this book were valid at the time of going to press.
However, due to the dynamic nature of the Internet, some addresses may have changed, or
sites may have changed or ceased to exist since publication. While the author and
Publishers regret any inconvenience this may cause readers, no responsibility for any such
changes can be accepted by either the author or the Publishers.

Index

Titles in the *How Do They Work?* series include:

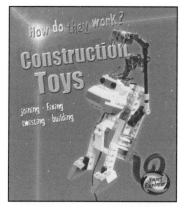

Hardback   0 431 04964 5

Hardback   0 431 04965 3

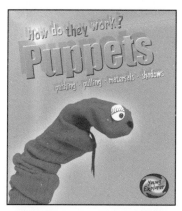

Hardback   0 431 04966 1

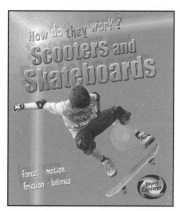

Hardback   0 431 04969 6

Hardback   0 431 04967 X

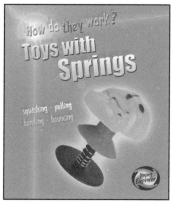

Hardback   0 431 04968 8

Find out about the other titles in this series on our website www.heinemann.co.uk/library